CW00374975

THE BIG

50

Your Survival Guide

An exclusive edition for

for all your gift books and gift stationery

This edition first published in Great Britain in 2018 by
Allsorted Ltd, Watford, Herts, UK WD19 4BG

All rights reserved. No part of this work may be reproduced in
any form or by any means, electronic or mechanical, including
photocopying, recording or by any information storage and
retrieval system, without the prior written permission of
the publisher.

© Susanna Geoghegan Gift Publishing

Author: Emma Hill

Cover design: Milestone Creative

ISBN: 978-1-911517-50-4

Printed in China

THE BIG 50 IS UPON YOU!

What to do with the next decade of your life? Firstly, you could dip into this book filled with witticisms, truths, jokes and advice on turning 50. Sure, we can look back on your 30s and 40s with wistful nostalgia; those heady days when you managed to buy clothes without first checking the washing label, but mostly we're looking ahead with optimism and enthusiasm, comfortable in our own skin, definitely wiser and ready to embark on a mid-life adventure. Don't let getting older drag you down (who knows how long it will take you to get back up again), embrace your fabulous fifties and let life begin!

YOU KNOW YOU ARE 50 WHEN...

- You try to avoid 'friend requests' from your children's schoolmates on Facebook

- If you see an item of clothing you like and that fits right, you buy several of the same in different colours

- You sound just like your mother

- You've learned to surround yourself with the people who value the same things in life as you

- You enjoy gardening

- You've given up trying to change other people

- You hate crowds so much that you remind yourself of your own dad...or granddad

- You listen to 'The Archers'

- The clothes you wore as a teenager are now considered vintage

YOU STILL 'HANG UP' THE PHONE

OUR BIRTHDAYS ARE FEATHERS IN THE BROAD WING OF TIME.

JEAN PAUL RICHTER

A WORD FROM THE WISE

Forty is the old age of youth; fifty is the youth of old age.
Victor Hugo

My face carries all my memories. Why would I change them?
Diane von Furstenberg

It is not true that people stop pursuing dreams because they grow old, they grow old because they stop pursuing dreams.
Gabriel Garcia Marquez

There's nothing tragic about being fifty. Not unless you're trying to be twenty-five.
William Holden

He not busy being born is busy dying.
Bob Dylan

70s & 80s TRIVIA
(PART 1)

1. Which famous TV show, running from 1980 to 1985, featured a police force in the fictional town of Hartley in Lancashire?

2. What was the highest grossing film of the 70s?

3. Who was awarded the Nobel Peace Prize in 1979?

4. Which song contains the lyrics: 'we don't need no education, we don't need no thought control'?

5. Edwina Currie resigned over what food?

6. Who played Lord Melchett in the TV comedy series **Blackadder II**?

7. Who was Labour leader when Thatcher won her third election victory?

8. In February 1980, the first episode of the television series **Yes Minister** aired. It portrayed the political frustrations of which fictitious MP?

9. Who played the role of Sandy Olsson in the 1978 film Grease?

10. Which 1979 song by Art Garfunkel featured in the animated movie **Watership Down**?

(See page 94 for answers)

THINGS TO DO NOW YOU'RE 50

- Make a retirement plan
- Let your adventurous spirit out and go on an off-the-beaten-track holiday
- Acquire a hobby that brings you pleasure
- Forgive someone
- Teach someone how to do something you're really good at
- Throw a surprise party
- Celebrate New Year's Eve in a foreign city
- Get a custom dress or suit made
- Stop putting things off for 'some day'

GO
SCUBA DIVING

I TOLD MY WIFE THAT A MAN IS LIKE A FINE WINE... I ALWAYS GET BETTER WITH AGE

THE NEXT DAY, SHE LOCKED ME IN THE WINE CELLAR.

UNKNOWN

YOU'RE HAVING A LAUGH

Looking 50 is great - if you're 60.
Joan Rivers

Middle age is when your narrow waist and your broad mind change places.
Unknown

Your age is merely the number of years the world has been enjoying you.
Unknown

Setting a good example for your children takes all the fun out of middle age.
William Feather

She was a handsome woman of forty-five and would remain so for many years.
Anita Brookner

I FIND AS I GROW OLDER THAT I LOVE THOSE MOST WHOM I LOVED FIRST.

THOMAS JEFFERSON

A WORD FROM THE WISE

50 years: here's a time when you have to separate yourself from what other people expect of you, and do what you love. Because if you find yourself 50 years old and you aren't doing what you love, then what's the point?
Jim Carrey

You are as young as your faith, as old as your doubt, as young as your self-confidence, as old as your fear, as young as your hope and as old as your despair.
Douglas MacArthur

The process of maturing is an art to be learned, an effort to be sustained. By the age of fifty you have made yourself what you are, and if it is good, it is better than your youth.
Marya Mannes

The golden age is before us, not behind us.
William Shakespeare

DID YOU KNOW?

Several studies support the notion that the mid-life crisis is a myth; that in fact the trajectory of happiness and contentment is a straight line going up. Put simply, the older you get, the happier you get.

Once a man reaches the age of 50, he will find that there are more women in the world of his own age than men; below 50, the reverse is true.

Once you've hit 50, you're more likely to experience job satisfaction. In one study, 92 per cent of workers aged 50 or older reported being very or somewhat satisfied with their job. Compare that with those under 30 - only 80 per cent of this group reported the same thing.

A HIGH SUGAR DIET HAS BEEN SHOWN TO INCREASE THE RISK OF CHRONIC DISEASE AND CAN LEAVE OUR SKIN DULL AND WRINKLED BEFORE ITS TIME.

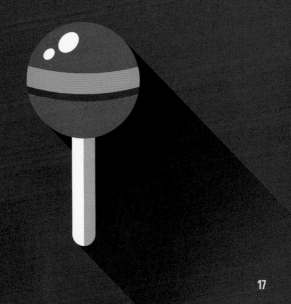

50 THINGS YOU SHOULD KNOW BY THE TIME YOU TURN 50 (PART 1)

- Life isn't fair...that doesn't mean it can't be good

- Wear Factor 50...every day

- Envy is a waste of time

- How to see the bigger picture

- There is nothing more important than spending quality time with your family

- Success is to love and be loved

- How to appreciate the small things...that are actually the big things

- How to save money

- Current circumstances are fleeting

CANDLELIGHT IS YOUR FRIEND

YOU'RE NEVER TOO OLD

At 51, the Marquis de Sade wrote the novel **Justine**.

Emperor Claudius was 50 years old when he became Rome's leader. Many expected him to be a weak ruler but he completed the Roman conquest of Britain and went on to rule for 13 years.

Jack Cover invented the Taser gun – named after a Tom Swift novel – aged 50.

Actress Kathryn Joosten, who won two Emmys for her work on **Desperate Housewives**, moved to Hollywood at the age of 56 to become an actress.

AT 52, SIR FRANCIS CHICHESTER SAILED AROUND THE WORLD ALONE IN A 53-FOOT BOAT NORMALLY MANNED BY A CREW OF SIX.

YOU KNOW YOU ARE 50 WHEN...

- You look at the washing instructions before you buy an item of clothing

- You wish you hadn't thrown out your old toys that are now worth thousands of pounds

- You feed the birds

- When you're giving someone your email address you still say 'all one word, in lowercase'

- You buy over-the-counter reading glasses...

- ...and then wear them around your neck

- You become a 'Friend' of iconic establishments

- Technology stops making sense

- You never go out without your coat

YOU HAVE TO GET UP IN THE NIGHT TO USE THE BATHROOM... AT LEAST ONCE

LIFE IS SHORT, BUY THE SHOES.

UNKNOWN

A WORD FROM THE WISE

No wise man ever wished to be younger.
Jonathan Swift

No book is really worth reading at the age of ten which is not equally - and often far more - worth reading at the age of fifty and beyond.
C.S. Lewis

And in the end, it's not the years in your life that count. It's the life in your years.
Abraham Lincoln

We age not by years, but by stories.
Maza-Dohta

We try to achieve beauty by covering up all traces of age and end up looking like we tried to achieve youth by covering up all traces of beauty.
Robert Brault

70s & 80s TRIVIA
(PART 2)

1. Which company, now one of the world's most valuable, was formed in 1975?

2. Who had a 'Heart of Glass' in 1979?

3. Student-led demonstrations in China took place in which square?

4. What was the name of the car in the Dukes of Hazzard?

5. Which questionable 80s hairstyle was long at the back, short at the sides?

6. In 1985, who purchased the London department store Harrods?

7. Who did John Hinckley attempt to assassinate in 1981?

8. The development of Concorde was a joint project between France and which other country?

9. In 1978, who became the first man in history to score a century and take eight wickets in one innings of Test Match Cricket?

10. What were the two types of VCR that competed against each other for much of the 80s?

(See page 95 for answers)

THINGS TO DO NOW YOU'RE 50

- Support a charity
- Perform random acts of kindness
- Visit the places where your parents grew up
- Master public speaking
- Research your family history
- Repair something by yourself
- Ignore the trends and wear what suits you
- Go on holiday in an exotic country
- Become an expert in something

HAVE A MEAL IN ONE OF THE WORLD'S TOP RESTAURANTS

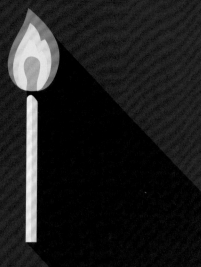

DON'T THINK OF IT AS
GETTING HOT FLUSHES. THINK
OF IT AS YOUR INNER CHILD
PLAYING WITH MATCHES.

UNKNOWN

YOU'RE HAVING A LAUGH

When you are dissatisfied and would like to go back to youth, think of algebra.
Will Rogers

Maybe it's true that life begins at fifty. But everything else starts to wear out, fall out, or spread out.
Phyllis Diller

The older you get the stronger the wind gets - and it's always in your face.
Jack Nicklaus

Middle age: That time when you finally get your head together - but then your body starts falling apart.
Unknown

Memory is the first casualty of middle age, if I remember correctly.
Candice Bergen

50 THINGS YOU SHOULD KNOW BY THE TIME YOU TURN 50 (PART 2)

- Relationships take compromise

- Rules are only guidelines

- How to enjoy your own company

- Respect is earned

- To make yourself a priority

- Smile and the world smiles with you

- There is more to life than work

- When someone starts a sentence with 'I'm not being...' they always are

- You're not entitled to anything...you have to work for everything you want

DON'T FORGET TO FLOSS

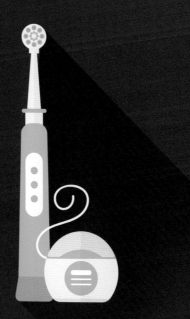

AT MIDDLE AGE THE SOUL SHOULD BE OPENING UP LIKE A ROSE, NOT CLOSING UP LIKE A CABBAGE.

JOHN ANDREW HOLMES

A WORD FROM THE WISE

For what it's worth: it's never too late to be whoever you want to be. I hope you live a life you're proud of, and if you find that you're not, I hope you have the strength to start over.
F. Scott Fitzgerald

The older I get, the less I know. It's wonderful – it makes the world so spacious.
Swami Chetanananda

Life's tragedy is that we get old too soon and wise too late.
Benjamin Franklin

How old would you be if you didn't know how old you are?
Satchel Paige

Live not one's life as though one had a thousand years, but live each day as the last.
Marcus Aurelius

RAY KROC SPENT HIS CAREER AS A MILKSHAKE DEVICE SALESMAN BEFORE BUYING MCDONALD'S AT THE AGE OF 52 AND GROWING IT INTO THE WORLD'S BIGGEST FAST-FOOD FRANCHISE.

YOU'RE NEVER TOO OLD

Miguel de Cervantes was in his late 50s when he wrote his seminal novel Don Quixote.

At age 50, Barbra Streisand won a 10-year film and recording contract estimated to be worth $60 million.

At 53, Ludwig van Beethoven completed his Ninth Symphony.

Paul Cézanne had his first art exhibition aged 56. He went on to produce such masterpieces as Pyramid of Skulls and The Bathers.

YOU KNOW YOU ARE 50 WHEN...

- Your kids' social lives are far livelier than yours... and you like it that way

- You phone people more than you text them

- You grunt when you put on your socks

- You hear teenagers talking and have no idea what they're saying

- Modern music all sounds the same to you

- You get nostalgic about the 'good old days'

- You carry a handy packet of tissues with you wherever you go

- You wear slippers at every given opportunity

- You've never taken a photograph of your food and posted it on Instagram

THE BEST THING ABOUT A SUNNY DAY IS THAT YOU CAN HANG THE WASHING OUT

A WORD FROM THE WISE

What I've learned in this first 50 is that if you can allow yourself to breathe into the depth, wonder, beauty, craziness, and strife - everything that represents the fullness of your life - you can live fearlessly. Because you come to realise that if you just keep breathing, you cannot be conquered.
Oprah Winfrey

You can't help getting older but you don't have to get old.
George Burns

With mirth and laughter let old wrinkles come.
William Shakespeare

Be sure to taste your words before you spit them out.
Unknown

None are so old as those who have outlived enthusiasm.
Henry David Thoreau

SOME PEOPLE, NO MATTER HOW OLD THEY GET, NEVER LOSE THEIR BEAUTY – THEY MERELY MOVE IT FROM THEIR FACES INTO THEIR HEARTS.

MARTIN BUXBAUM

THINGS TO DO NOW YOU'RE 50

- Take part in a race
- Become a mentor
- Visit a foreign city alone
- Clear the clutter - mental and physical - from your life
- Pay off your credit cards
- Write a will
- Learn another language
- Write in a journal
- Quit the job you hate

RIDE AN ELEPHANT

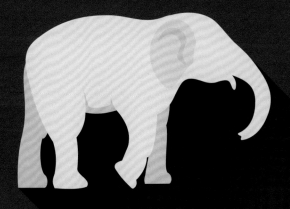

MIDDLE AGE IS WHEN YOU STILL BELIEVE YOU'LL FEEL BETTER IN THE MORNING.

BOB HOPE

YOU'RE HAVING A LAUGH

Age is just a number. It's totally irrelevant unless, of course, you happen to be a bottle of wine.
Joan Collins

Age is just a number...that changes depending on who's asking.

In a man's middle years there is scarcely a part of the body he would hesitate to turn over to the proper authorities.
E.B. White

When you get to fifty-two food becomes more important than sex.
Prue Leith

AS YOU GET OLDER, YOU GET FEWER COLDS. ON AVERAGE, ONCE YOU HIT 50 YOU'LL CATCH BETWEEN ONE AND TWO COLDS A YEAR COMPARED TO THE THREE 18 TO 35 YEAR OLDS ARE LIKELY TO SUFFER FROM.

DID YOU KNOW?

Research shows that our perceptions of ageing could be having a powerful affect on us. A study from Yale University and the University of California, Berkeley found that people who were exposed to positive stereotypes about ageing did better on physical tasks, such as balance, than their peers who had worked out for the previous six months.

Age spots are actually 'sun spots'. They have very little to do with the passing of time and are instead caused by too much exposure to sunshine.

Statistics show that a man aged 50 has an 11 per cent chance of living to the age of 100. A woman aged 50 has a 17 per cent chance of reaching 100.

22.6 per cent of the people on earth are over 50.

50 THINGS YOU SHOULD KNOW BY THE TIME YOU TURN 50 (PART 3)

- There is no reason to live the life others expect of you

- Not to keep the good china for best

- You can voice your own opinion without having to change someone else's

- You have the power to make yourself happy

- What suits you

- Nobody else controls you

- Not to compare yourself to others

- Long-term love is about trust, intimacy and feeling secure

- The value of old friends

HOW TO MIX A MARTINI

AGED 51, JOSEPH GUILLOTIN PROPOSED A BEHEADING MACHINE TO THE FRENCH NATIONAL ASSEMBLY.

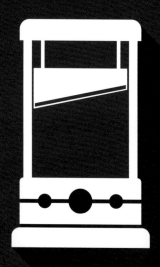

YOU'RE NEVER TOO OLD

Charles Darwin published **On the Origin of Species** aged 50, changing the scientific community forever.

At 58, Jacob Perkins created a compression machine, paving the way for the invention of gas refrigeration.

Sue Monk Kidd published her first novel, **The Secret Life of Bees**, aged 53.

At 59, Einstein achieved a major new result in the general theory of relativity.

YOU KNOW YOU ARE 50 WHEN...

- You don't know any of the songs in the top ten

- You have a landline

- You take a keen interest in dressing for the weather

- You pick places to go based on the ambient noise level

- You have hairs sprouting out of your chin (and you're a woman)

- Your back hurts for no reason

- Buying a new appliance makes you happy

- Some of your friends' children are getting married

- You start to think dessert wine is acceptable

YOU HAVE TO PUT YOUR GLASSES ON TO READ THE MENU

70s & 80s TRIVIA
(PART 3)

1. Who insisted 'I'm Not In Love' in 1975?

2. In 1976, Anita Roddick opened the first branch of which environmentally conscious store?

3. The first commercial CD players were introduced by which two companies in 1984?

4. In what year did Argentina invade the Falkland Islands?

5. What was the name of the once Morrissey-fronted 80s band?

6. In 1976, an American panel warned the world that using what causes damage to the ozone layer?

7. The first of only 12 episodes of which cult TV comedy series aired in the UK in 1975?

8. Which video game console was released in October 1977?

9. Which Spaniard won two US Masters in the 80s?

10. Of which song was it said that 'Three and a half minutes of melodramatic caterwauling is always better than 300 pages of melodramatic prose'?

(See page 95 for answers)

THE KEY TO AGEING SUCCESSFULLY IS TO PAY AS LITTLE ATTENTION TO IT AS POSSIBLE.

UNKNOWN

A WORD FROM THE WISE

There's nothing stressful about turning 50 except people reminding you about it.
Muhammad Ali

Every age can be enchanting, provided you live within it.
Bridgette Bardot

Youth is a circumstance you can't do anything about. The trick is to grow up without getting old.
Frank Lloyd Wright

Whatever with the past has gone,
The best is always yet to come.
Lucy Larcom

THINGS TO DO NOW YOU'RE 50

- Revisit your honeymoon destination
- Find your theme tune
- Conquer your fears
- Go on safari
- Volunteer your time and skills
- Take a job that's out of your comfort zone
- Get in touch with an old school friend
- Dye your hair a different colour
- Go skinny-dipping

SING KARAOKE

YOU KNOW YOU'RE GETTING OLDER WHEN IT TAKES LONGER TO REST THAN IT DID TO GET TIRED.

UNKNOWN

YOU'RE HAVING A LAUGH

If you haven't grown up by age 50, you don't have to.
Unknown

An archaeologist is the best husband a woman can have. The older she gets the more interested he is in her.
Agatha Christie

Children are a great comfort in your old age - and they help you to reach it faster, too.
Lionel Kauffman

For 50, you look great! Of course I don't have my glasses on.

Middle age - later than you think and sooner than you expect.
Earl Wilson

I DON'T BELIEVE IN AGEING. I BELIEVE IN FOREVER ALTERING ONE'S ASPECT TO THE SUN.

VIRGINIA WOOLF

A WORD FROM THE WISE

If you are 50 you're never going to be 50 ever again so enjoy being 50. If you sit through the year wishing you were younger, before you know it it's going to be over and you're going to be 51.
Julianne Moore

By the time we hit 50, we have learned our hardest lessons. We have found out that only a few things are really important. We have learned to take life seriously, but never ourselves.
Marie Dressler

Some day you will be old enough to start reading fairy tales again.
C.S. Lewis

At 50, everyone has the face he deserves.
George Orwell

There is a certain part of all of us that lives outside of time. Perhaps we become aware of our age only at exceptional moments and most of the time we are ageless.
Milan Kundera

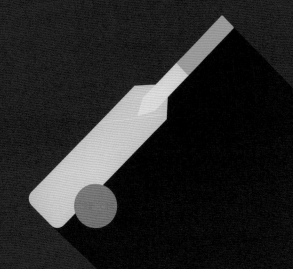

W. G. GRACE, WILFRED RHODES AND GEORGE GUNN ALL PLAYED CRICKET FOR ENGLAND AFTER THEIR 50TH BIRTHDAYS.

DID YOU KNOW?

Your personality is probably improving! A study from psychologists at the University of California found that conscientiousness and agreeableness (warmth, generosity and helpfulness) are personality traits that improve with age.

According to the Office of National Statistics, someone in the UK turns 50 every 40 seconds.

You are probably now more level headed and less emotional - our bodies make less adrenaline, testosterone and oestrogen as we age, evening out our emotions and making us calmer and more even-tempered.

50 THINGS YOU SHOULD KNOW BY THE TIME YOU TURN 50 (PART 4)

- Cheap wine is not for you
- If you don't ask, you don't get
- How to live within your means
- How to stay open to change
- It's easier to be positive than negative
- Worrying is a waste of time
- To embrace new challenges
- Optimism is contagious
- To question the status quo

HOW TO GET AROUND IN A FOREIGN COUNTRY

INVENTOR WALTER HUNT PATENTED THE SAFETY PIN AGED 53.

YOU'RE NEVER TOO OLD

Abraham Lincoln was elected president of the United States aged 52 (after having lost a congressional race at the age of 34; losing a senatorial race at the age of 45; failing in an effort to become vice-president aged 47; and losing a senatorial race at the age of 49. That's perseverance!).

Pablo Picasso completed his masterpiece, Guernica, when he was 55.

At the age of 53, Jimmy Carter facilitated the Camp David accords between Israel and Egypt.

Long-time dissident Vaclav Havel became president of Czechoslovakia aged 53.

YOU KNOW YOU ARE 50 WHEN...

- You check the menu online and make your selections before you've even arrived at the restaurant

- You replace the adjective 'fun' with 'tiring', as in that party sounds 'tiring'...

- Loud music that isn't yours bothers you

- You prefer a Sunday stroll to a lie-in

- You own scented drawer liners

- You don't understand Instagram or Snapchat

- When you get a new mobile phone you ask your kids to set it up for you

- You buy relaxed-fit jeans

- You forget where you parked your car

YOU SELECT YOUR SHOES FOR COMFORT NOT STYLE

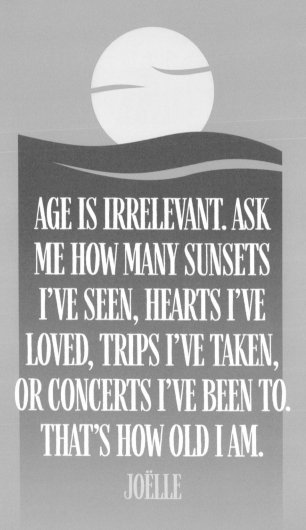

AGE IS IRRELEVANT. ASK
ME HOW MANY SUNSETS
I'VE SEEN, HEARTS I'VE
LOVED, TRIPS I'VE TAKEN,
OR CONCERTS I'VE BEEN TO.
THAT'S HOW OLD I AM.

JOËLLE

A WORD FROM THE WISE

A man who views the world the same at fifty as he did at twenty has wasted thirty years of his life.
Muhammad Ali

Youthfulness is about how you live not when you were born.
Karl Lagerfeld

I love my age. Old enough to know better. Young enough not to care. Experienced enough to do it right.
Unknown

I have enjoyed greatly the second blooming... suddenly you find at the age of 50, say - that a whole new life has opened before you.
Agatha Christie

Age does not protect you from love. But love, to some extent, protects you from age.
Anaïs Nin

RESEARCH BY NUTRITIONAL SCIENTISTS SUGGESTS A STRONG LINK BETWEEN HEALTHY NUTRITION AND OUR HEALTH AS WE AGE. A HEALTHY DIET SHOULD INCLUDE FRUITS, VEGETABLES AND LEGUMES TO GET ALL THE ANTIOXIDANTS WE NEED TO REDUCE THE CELLULAR EFFECTS OF AGEING.

DID YOU KNOW?

Contrary to the stereotypical image of getting grumpy and lonely as we age, research shows that anger declines steadily from our 20s through our 70s and stress falls off a cliff in our 50s.

The first recorded use of the term 'silver surfer' for an over-50 browsing the Internet was in 1997.

Stanley Matthews turned 50 on 1st February, 1965. It was five days later that he became the only over 50 to play in the top division of English football.

THINGS TO DO NOW YOU'RE 50

- Participate in a peaceful protest

- Enrol in an evening class

- Nurture your curiosities

- Do something that scares you

- Sleep under the stars

- See the Northern Lights

- Take a martial arts class

- Make (and stick to) a budget

- Volunteer in a homeless shelter

LEARN TO SALSA DANCE

AGE 50! NOW IS THE TIME TO MAKE YOUR MARK ON THE WORLD – EXPLORE THE ANTARCTIC OR BECOME AN ASTRONAUT. MAKE YOUR MIND UP TO TAKE ON EXCITING NEW CHALLENGES –STRAIGHT AFTER YOUR AFTERNOON NAP.

UNKNOWN

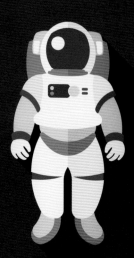

YOU'RE HAVING A LAUGH

Middle age: When you begin to exchange your emotions for symptoms.
Irvin S Cobb

When I wished for a smoking hot body, menopause was not quite what I had in mind.
Unknown

Whatever you may look like, marry a man your own age – as your beauty fades, so will his eyesight.
Phyllis Diller

Middle age is when you're sitting at home on a Saturday night and the telephone rings and you hope it isn't for you.
Ogden Nash

A true friend remembers your birthday but not your age.
Unknown

WITH AGE COMES WISDOM, BUT SOMETIMES AGE COMES ALONE.

OSCAR WILDE

A WORD FROM THE WISE

Nature gives you the face you have at twenty; it is up to you to merit the face you have at fifty.
Coco Chanel

I look forward to being older, when what you look like becomes less and less an issue and what you are is the point.
Susan Sarandon

In youth we learn; in age we understand.
Marie von Ebner-Eschenbach

A beautiful face will age and a perfect body will change, but a beautiful soul will always be a beautiful soul.
Unknown

The older you get, the more important it is to not act your age.
Ashleigh Brilliant

YOU'RE NEVER TOO OLD

Mao Zedong founded the People's Republic of China aged 56

Sony chairman Akio Morita introduced the Sony Walkman, an idea no one seemed to like at the time, aged 58.

At the age of 54, Henry Heimlich developed his emergency manoeuvre.

It was at the age of 57 that Kathryn Bigelow attained international success when she made The Hurt Locker.

AT 57, FRANK DOBESH COMPETED IN HIS FIRST 100-MILE BICYCLE RIDE – 10 YEARS AFTER HE WAS DIAGNOSED WITH AN INOPERABLE BRAIN TUMOUR.

50 THINGS YOU SHOULD KNOW BY THE TIME YOU TURN 50 (PART 5)

- How to listen, really listen
- How to negotiate
- Compassion is key
- They're not a bargain if they're two sizes too small
- How to ask for a promotion
- Be kind
- There's no such thing as a grown-up...we're all big kids just playing at it
- How to accept a compliment
- To make your needs a priority

HOW TO BUILD A FIRE

THINGS TO DO NOW YOU'RE 50

- Organise your wardrobe

- Go on a road trip with friends

- Start a blog

- Ride in a hot air balloon

- Visit relatives abroad

- Write a short story

- Take a singing lesson or join a choir

- Complete a physical challenge

- Adopt a personal mantra

EAT DESSERT
FOR BREAKFAST

70s & 80s TRIVIA
(PART 4)

1. How many countries boycotted the Summer Olympics held in Moscow in 1980 and why?

2. What was the first portable stereo, introduced by Sony in 1978, known as?

3. Who was elected President of the United States in 1980?

4. The answer was 'Kristen'. But what was the question?

5. In what year did France perform its last execution by guillotine?

6. Who was the voice of 'Willo The Wisp'?

7. Which British comedian suffered a heart attack on live television, and died soon after, in April 1984?

8. In which year did Bucks Fizz win the Eurovision Song Contest with 'Making Your Mind Up'?

9. Which classic arcade game was released in Japan on 22nd May 1980?

10. Duran Duran derived their name from a character in which classic sci-fi film?

(See page 96 for answers)

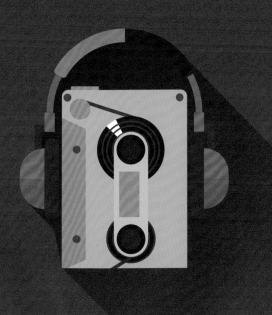

YOU'RE NEVER TOO OLD

John Pemberton was 55 when he came up with the formula for Coca-Cola.

Taikichiro Mori left academia aged 55 to pursue a career in Tokyo real estate. He subsequently became the richest man in the world with a net worth of around $13 billion.

Ronald Reagan was 55 when he entered politics.

It wasn't until Vivienne Westwood's 50th birthday that the world really took notice of her, thanks to the now iconic Mini Crini skirt.

AT 54, ANNIE JUMP CANNON BECAME THE FIRST ASTRONOMER TO CLASSIFY THE STARS ACCORDING TO SPECTRAL TYPE.

SOME PEOPLE ARE OLD AT 18 AND SOME ARE YOUNG AT 90...TIME IS A CONCEPT THAT HUMANS CREATED.

YOKO ONO

A WORD FROM THE WISE

Probably the happiest period in life most frequently is in middle age, when the eager passions of youth are cooled, and the infirmities of age not yet begun; as we see that the shadows, which are at morning and evening so large, almost entirely disappear at midday.
Eleanor Roosevelt

Some age, others mature.
Sean Connery

Live your life and forget your age.
Norman Vincent Peale

Wrinkles mean you lived, grey hairs mean you cared and scars mean you lived.
Unknown

It's never too early to age elegantly.
Unknown

ANSWERS: 70s & 80s TRIVIA

(PART 1)

1. Juliet Bravo

2. Star Wars

3. Mother Theresa

4. 'Another Brick In The Wall' by Pink Floyd

5. Eggs

6. Stephen Fry

7. Neil Kinnock

8. Jim Hacker

9. Olivia Newton-John

10. 'Bright Eyes'

(PART 2)

1. Microsoft
2. Blondie
3. Tiananmen Square
4. General Lee
5. The mullet
6. Mohammed Al Fayed
7. President Reagan
8. Britain
9. Ian Botham
10. VHS & Betamax

(PART 3)

1. 10cc
2. The Body Shop
3. Sony and Philips
4. 1982
5. The Smiths

6. Aerosol cans, due to CFCs (Chlorofluorocarbons)

7. Fawlty Towers

8. Atari 2600

9. Seve Ballesteros

10. 'Wuthering Heights' by Kate Bush

(PART 4)

1. Sixty-five, to protest against the Soviet invasion of Afghanistan

2. The Walkman

3. Ronald Reagan

4. Who shot JR?

5. 1977

6. Kenneth Williams

7. Tommy Cooper

8. 1981

9. Pac-Man

10. Barbarella